O9-BUB-543

Consultants:

The Right Reverend Clarence N. Coleridge, Bishop
Episcopal Diocese of Connecticut

Reverend Monsignor Thomas J. Driscoll, Chancellor
Diocese of Bridgeport, Connecticut

Rabbi Charles A. Kroloff, D.D.
Temple Emanu-El, Westfield, New Jersey

A Reader's Digest Young Families Book
Published by Joshua Morris Publishing, Inc.,
355 Riverside Avenue, Westport, CT 06880.

ISBN: 0-89577-815-7
10 9 8 7 6 5 4 3 2

Originally published as *La Bible: Les belles histoires de l'Ancien et du Nouveau Testament.*

Library of Congress Cataloging in Publication Data

Delval, Marie-Hélène.
[Bible. English]
Reader's Digest Bible for children: timeless stories from the Old and New Testaments/ stories retold by Marie-Hélène Delval; illustrations by Ulises Wensell; foreword by Joni Eareckson Tada; [translated by Ronnie Apter and Mark Herman].
p. cm.
Translation of: La Bible: les belles histoires de l'Ancien et du Nouveau Testament.
Summary: An illustrated collection of Bible stories from both the Old and New Testaments.
ISBN 0-89577-815-7
1. Bible stories, English. [1. Bible stories.] I. Wensell, Ulises, ill. II. Reader's Digest Association. III. Title.
BS551.2.D45 1995
220.9'505—dc20

95-7993
CIP
AC

READER'S DIGEST
Bible for Children

Timeless Stories from the Old and New Testaments

Stories retold by Marie-Hélène Delval
Illustrations by Ulises Wensell
Foreword by Joni Eareckson Tada

READER'S DIGEST YOUNG FAMILIES

TABLE OF CONTENTS

Stories from the Old Testament

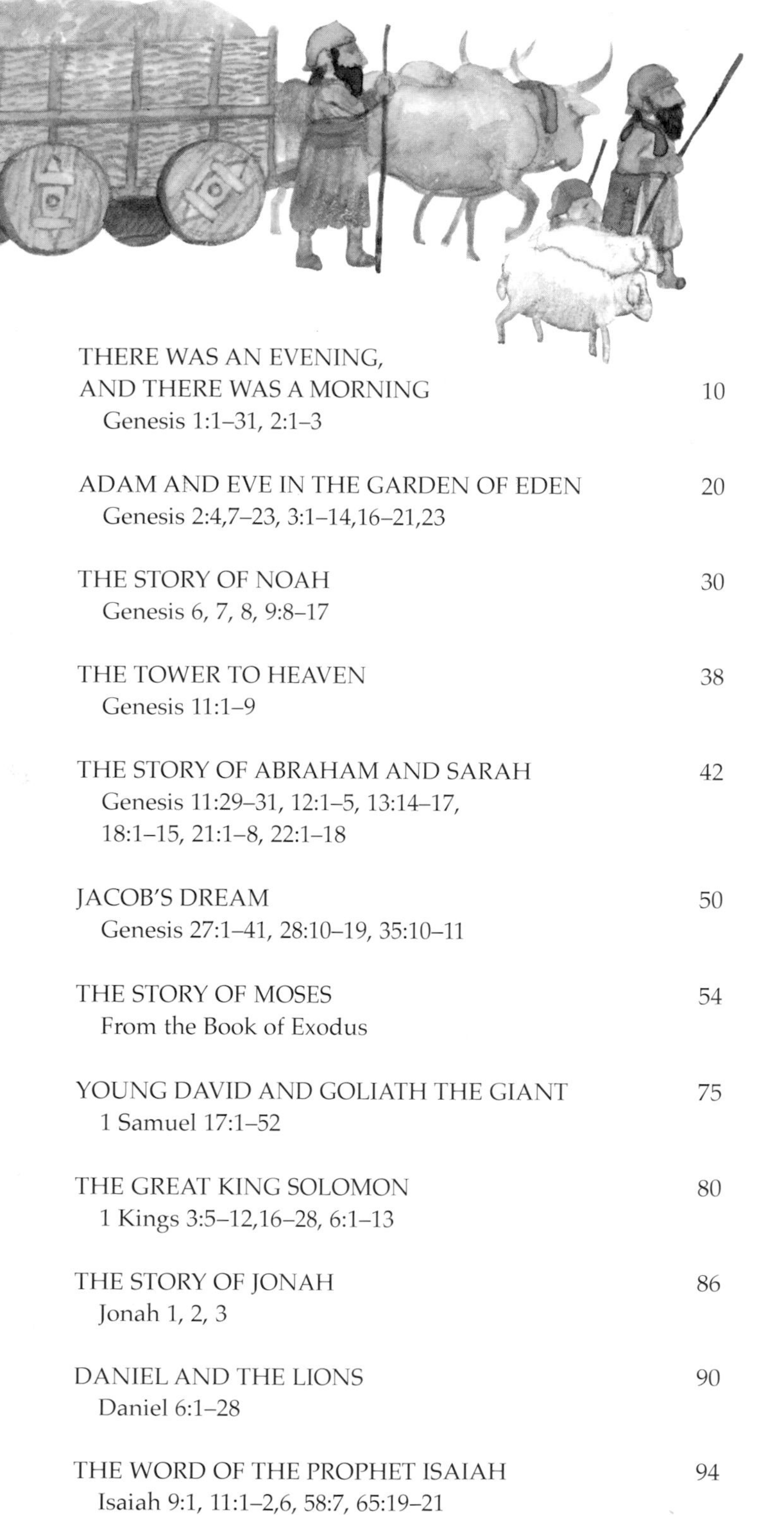

Stories from the New Testament

FOREWORD

I love adventure stories, whether they're about a shepherd boy who becomes a king, or a fisherman who drops everything to hunt for the meaning of life. That's why I love reading the Bible.

In these Bible stories, you'll learn the name of the wisest man who ever lived, and what happened to a man who landed in the belly of a fish. You'll go on a long hike with the people of Israel, and see how God led them over dry deserts and through dangerous, deep rivers. You'll hear about a plague of frogs and flies, and how a couple of fish and a few loaves of bread made lunch for thousands of hungry people.

So treasure the remarkable book you are about to explore. And when you read about wise men, shepherds and fishermen, when you meet Jesus, the Son of God, in the amazing stories of his life, ask God to teach you what he wants you to learn. And who knows? You may discover that you are on a marvelous adventure, and that your life, too, can be a story: an adventure story that will lead you right into the circle of God's closest friends.

Joni Eareckson Tada

Stories from
The Old Testament

There Was an Evening, and There Was a Morning

In the beginning
God created heaven and earth.
The earth was empty and covered by darkness,
and the Spirit of God floated over the waters.

God said, "Let there be light!"
And the light burst forth.
God saw that the light was good
and he called it "day"
and separated it from night.
There was an evening, and there was a morning,
and this was the first day.

God said, "Let the heavens separate
the waters below from the waters above."
And it was so.
There was an evening, and there was a morning.
This was the second day.

Then God said, "Let the waters below gather
into one place, so that there may be
both dry land and sea."
And God saw that it was good.

God said, "Let plants grow
and flower on the land.
Let trees grow and give fruit."
There was an evening, and there was a morning.
This was the third day.

God said, "Let the sun light up the day,
let the moon and stars brighten the night."
And God saw that it was good.
There was an evening, and there was a morning.
This was the fourth day.

God spoke again:
"Let birds fly in the sky,
let fish swim in the sea."
And God saw that it was good.
There was an evening, and there was a morning.
This was the fifth day.

God said, "Let creatures great and small
crawl and walk and run on the dry land."
Then God said, "I shall make men and women
in my own likeness.
They shall have children
and have the earth for their home,
all of the earth, which I shall give them."
And God made people in his own image.

God looked at all he had made
and saw that it was very good.
There was another evening,
and another morning.
This was the sixth day.

On the seventh day, God rested.
God blessed the seventh day
and made it holy, because
the work of creation was finished.

Adam and Eve in the Garden of Eden

After the creation
of heaven and earth,
God formed a man
from the dust of the ground.
God breathed the breath of life
into the man's nostrils,
and the man came alive.

God planted a wonderful
garden for the man,
and in the middle of the garden
God placed two trees:
the tree of life, and the tree that
gives knowledge of good and evil.

God said to the man, "You may eat fruit
from the trees in the garden.
But do not eat the fruit of the tree
that gives knowledge of good and evil.
If you eat it, you will die."

Then God said, "The man is alone,
and that is not good."
So God brought the animals of the fields
and the birds of the sky to the man,
so that he could name them.
But still he was alone.

Then God put the man into a deep sleep.
God took a rib from his chest,
and, from that rib, God formed a woman.
When the man saw the woman, he cried,
"Here is my partner, my helpmate!"

Now the snake was the slyest
of all the animals.
He said to the woman,
"So God has forbidden you
to eat fruit from the trees!"
The woman answered, "No,
we eat fruit from all the trees, except
the one in the middle of the garden.
God has told us, 'Do not touch it!
If you eat from it, you will die.' "
The snake replied,
"Not so! You will not die.
But God knows that if you eat its fruit,
you will have knowledge of good and evil
and will be like God yourselves."

The fruit of the tree was beautiful
and looked delicious.
The woman took one and ate it.
She gave some to her husband,
and he ate, too.

Suddenly their eyes were opened.
The man and the woman saw
that they were naked and unprotected,
and they made clothes from the leaves
of a fig tree to cover their bodies.

God came to walk in the garden.
When the man and the woman heard
God's voice, they hid behind trees.
God called to the man, "Where are you?"
The man answered,
"I am hiding because I am naked."
God said, "How do you know you are naked?
Have you eaten the fruit
of the forbidden tree?"
The man said, "The woman
you made for me offered me some!"
God said to the woman, "Why did you do this?"
And the woman answered,
"The snake tricked me!"

God said to the snake,
"Because you have done this,
you will be cursed.
You will crawl on your belly and eat the dirt."
God said to the man and the woman,
"Because you have eaten the fruit
of the forbidden tree,
you will know suffering,
and you will have to work hard
in order to feed yourselves.
Then you will die
and return to dust."

God clothed the man and the woman
in animal skins and told them to leave the garden.
The man, Adam, went away with his wife.
God called her Eve, which means "living,"
because she is the mother of all who are living.

The Story of Noah

Men and women increased in number,
multiplying throughout the earth,
and God saw that they were wicked.
God said, "I shall wipe them
from the face of the earth,
both humans and beasts,
all creatures great and small,
and even the birds in the sky,
for I am sorry that I made them."

But there was one good man.
His name was Noah
and he had three sons,
Shem, Ham, and Japheth.
God said to Noah, "Build an ark,
a great wooden boat,
and put a roof over it.
Go into the ark with your family,
and take with you a pair of
every kind of animal,
those that walk and those that crawl,
even the birds that fly.
For in seven days,
I shall make it rain on the earth
for forty days and forty nights."

Noah did what God told him to do.
He built a big ark, and into it he took his family
and two of every animal great and small,
even the birds of the sky.
And God shut the door behind him.

The rain fell and the waters climbed,
lifting the ark higher and higher.
The floods covered the entire earth,
even the highest mountains.
All things that lived on dry land perished.
Only Noah remained,
and those who were with him on the ark.

Days passed, but God had not forgotten Noah.
The rain stopped and the wind blew.
Slowly the waters began to subside,
and the ark came to rest on a mountaintop.
Noah waited forty days.
He released a raven, which flew back and forth
waiting for the waters to dry.
Then Noah released a dove,
which returned to the ark,
for she had found no place to set her feet.

Noah waited seven more days
and released the dove again.
In the evening, the dove returned.
In her beak, she was holding
a small olive branch,
and Noah knew the waters had gone down.
He waited seven more days.
Again he released the dove,
and this time she did not return.
Noah looked and saw that the land was dry.

At God's command, Noah left the ark
with his family and all the animals.
Then God said,
"Never again will I destroy the earth
because people are wicked!
So long as the earth lasts,
there will be sowing and reaping,
summer and winter, day and night."

And God said to Noah,
"Today, I make a promise, a covenant with you
and your children and your children's children.
Look! I have set a rainbow among the clouds.
It is the sign of my covenant
with all things living on the earth.
Never again will I send a flood to destroy them!"

The Tower to Heaven

After the flood,
people once again began to spread
over the face of the earth.
They were one people,
speaking the same language.
While traveling about with their flocks,
they discovered a large plain
where they could settle.

They said to each other,
"Let us make bricks and
fire them in the furnace
to build walls. Let us build a city
with a very high tower,
so high that it touches heaven,
and we will become great
and powerful!"

God came down to see the city and the tower
being built. And God said,
"How great and strong these people think they are!
But why do they seek to pierce the sky
when I have given them so many countries,
the whole earth, to live in?"

And so God confused their speech.
They could no longer understand each other.
They stopped building.
From that time on, the city was called Babel,
because the people there babbled
in different languages.
And the builders of Babel became
the many scattered peoples of the earth.

The Story of Abraham and Sarah

Abraham lived in the land of Haran
with his father, Terah, and all his family.
Abraham was an old man.
His wife, Sarah, was also old,
and she had never borne a child.
God said to Abraham,
"Leave your country,
your relatives, and the house of your father,
and go to the land that I will show you.
I will bless you, and I will make of you a great people."

Abraham believed the word of God.
He gathered his servants and his herds of animals,
and he left Haran with his wife, Sarah.
He set out on a very long journey.
When he was camped in Canaan, God said to Abraham,
"Lift your eyes to the north and the south,
as far east as the sunrise,
as far west as the sunset.
All the land that you see, I give to you,
to you and your children and your children's children,
for they will number as many as the stars in the sky."

Now God appeared to
Abraham as he was sitting
at the entrance to his tent.
Abraham looked up and saw
three men standing in the hot sun.
He told them, "Rest yourselves under this tree.
I shall have water brought to wash your feet."
Abraham had unleavened bread baked for his guests
and chose a young calf from his herd.

The travelers ate, and then they asked him,
"Where is Sarah, your wife?"
Abraham answered, "She is there in the tent."
"Next spring, Sarah will bear you a son,"
the travelers declared.
And when Sarah heard them, she laughed to herself,
for she was much too old to have a child.
But the Lord said, "Why did Sarah laugh?
Is anything impossible for God?"
Then Sarah was afraid. "I did not laugh," she said.
But God said, "Oh yes, you did!"

Sarah had a son as God had promised. They named him Isaac, which means "he laughs," and Sarah said, "The Lord has indeed given me cause to laugh! Who would have believed that in my old age I would give Abraham a son?"

Abraham held a great party so that everyone might rejoice at the birth of the child promised by God.

Isaac grew to be a young boy.
And there came a day
when God called Abraham.
"Here I am!" Abraham answered.
And God said to him,
"Take Isaac, your only son,
your son whom you love,
and go to the mountain
that I will show you.
There, you shall offer him to me."

Abraham rose early.
He loaded his donkey with firewood
and left with his son Isaac.
Isaac said to him, "Father,
I see you are bringing wood for the fire,
but where is the lamb for the sacrifice?"
Abraham answered,
"God knows where the lamb is, my son."
And so they walked together.

When Abraham arrived on the mountaintop,
he built an altar and prepared the fire.
But as he grasped the knife,
the angel of God called to him from heaven,
"Abraham, Abraham!"
"I am here!" he answered.
And the angel told him,
"Do not harm your son!
I now know that you revere the Lord above all else!"
Looking around, Abraham saw a ram
with its horns tangled in a bush,
and he offered the ram in sacrifice.

Again the angel of God called to Abraham, saying,
"Because you have done this, God will bless you.
Your children's children will number as many
as the stars in the sky and the grains of sand by the sea.
All peoples of the earth will remember you."

Jacob's Dream

Jacob was the son of Isaac
and the grandson of Abraham.
He had a twin brother, Esau.
One day Jacob tricked his father
into giving him a blessing that had
been promised to Esau.
Esau became so angry that he planned
to kill his brother.
When Jacob found out about Esau's plan, he left
the house of his father for another country.
He walked an entire day.
As night was falling, he lay down against
a stone and fell asleep on that very spot.

Then Jacob had a dream:
he saw a ladder going up from the earth
until its top touched heaven.
God's angels were moving up and down the ladder.
And Jacob heard the voice of the Lord saying,
"I am the God of Abraham and Isaac.
The land on which you lie
I shall give to you,
to you and your children and your children's children.
They shall fill the earth, and they shall be blessed.
I am with you and will not desert you."
Jacob awoke.
He was afraid, and he cried out,
"How wonderful is this place!
Truly the Lord is here,
and I did not know it.
This place is a house of God, the door to heaven!"

Jacob took the stone on which he had slept
and set it up as a memorial.
And he called that place Bethel,
which means "the house of God."

Later, God said to Jacob,
"Your name shall no longer be Jacob, but Israel,
and you shall be the father of many nations."

The Story of Moses

In those days,
the children of Israel lived in Egypt
where they were called Hebrews.
They became so numerous and powerful
that the pharaoh, the king of Egypt, feared them.
He commanded that they work as slaves,
making bricks and building cities.
But still the Hebrews grew in number.
So the pharaoh commanded
that every newborn Hebrew boy
be put to death by drowning in the river Nile.

One woman had just given birth to a little boy.
She hid him for three months.
When she could hide him no longer,
she laid him in a basket and set the basket
among the rushes at the river's edge.
The baby's older sister hid nearby
to watch over him.

Now the pharaoh's daughter
came down to the river to bathe.
She saw the basket and sent
a serving girl to bring it to her.
The pharaoh's daughter looked at the baby boy,
who was crying.
She said, "It is a Hebrew child!"
and took pity on him.

The baby's sister, who had seen all this,
said to the pharaoh's daughter, "If you like,
I can find someone to nurse the baby."
And she went to find her mother.
So the mother nursed her own child,
and when he was older, the pharaoh's daughter
took him into the palace as her son.
She named him Moses, which means
"rescued from the waters."

Moses grew up in the pharaoh's palace.
But one day, he saw an Egyptian
beating a Hebrew man again and again.
And Moses killed the Egyptian.
The pharaoh learned of it and
meant to have Moses put to death.
But Moses fled from Egypt into the land of Midian
and became a shepherd.

One day, as he led his flock through the wilderness,
Moses came to Horeb, the mountain of God.
There he saw flames
spurting forth from a bush.
And, wonder of wonders,
the bush burned and burned
but did not turn to ashes.
Moses went closer.
From out of the bush, God spoke to him.
"Moses, Moses!
I have seen the suffering of my people.
I have heard their cries.
I will deliver them from the Egyptians.
Tell the pharaoh to let the
children of Israel go.
I am God, and I shall be with you!"

Moses returned to Egypt and his people.
He spoke to the pharaoh, but the pharaoh refused to listen.
Instead, he commanded that the
Hebrews be made to work even harder.
God told Moses to strike the Nile with his shepherd's crook,
and the Nile became a river of blood.
But the pharaoh still refused to let the Hebrews go.

God told Moses to raise his staff again,
and Egypt was invaded by frogs,
then by gnats, and then by flies.
But the pharaoh still refused
to let the Hebrews go.
Then God caused all the livestock
of the Egyptians to die.
God sent sickness,
then hailstorms, and then locusts.
Still the pharaoh refused.

God told Moses to raise his hand up to the sky,
and there came upon the land of Egypt
three days of darkest night.
But the pharaoh kept refusing,
for his heart was hardened.

Then God said to Moses,
"Tonight I shall strike Egypt,
and every firstborn in the land shall die,
both human and animal.
And the pharaoh will let you go.

Tonight, let each Hebrew family take a lamb
and eat its roasted flesh
with unleavened bread and bitter herbs.
You will eat standing up, your sandals on your feet,
and in great haste, for tonight is the Passover of the Lord!

You will mark the doors of your houses
with the blood of the lamb.
When I see this mark, I will pass over you,
and your houses will be spared the suffering
that will fall on the land of Egypt.
You will remember this night.
And you and your children and your children's children
will celebrate it forever."

That night, throughout Egypt, there was weeping and wailing. And the pharaoh ordered the Hebrews to leave the country.

The Hebrews left the land of Egypt,
and God led them to the Red Sea.
God went before to guide them,
as a pillar of cloud by day
and as a pillar of fire by night.

But the pharaoh's heart hardened once again.
He took his horses, his chariots, and his riders,
and he pursued the children of Israel.
When the Hebrews saw the Egyptians coming,
they became very afraid.

Then God said to Moses,
"Raise high your shepherd's crook,
stretch your hand over the sea, and split it in two!"

Moses stretched his hand over the sea.
God caused a powerful wind to blow,
and the waters parted.
The Hebrews walked through the middle
of the sea on dry ground,
with high walls of water to the right and the left.

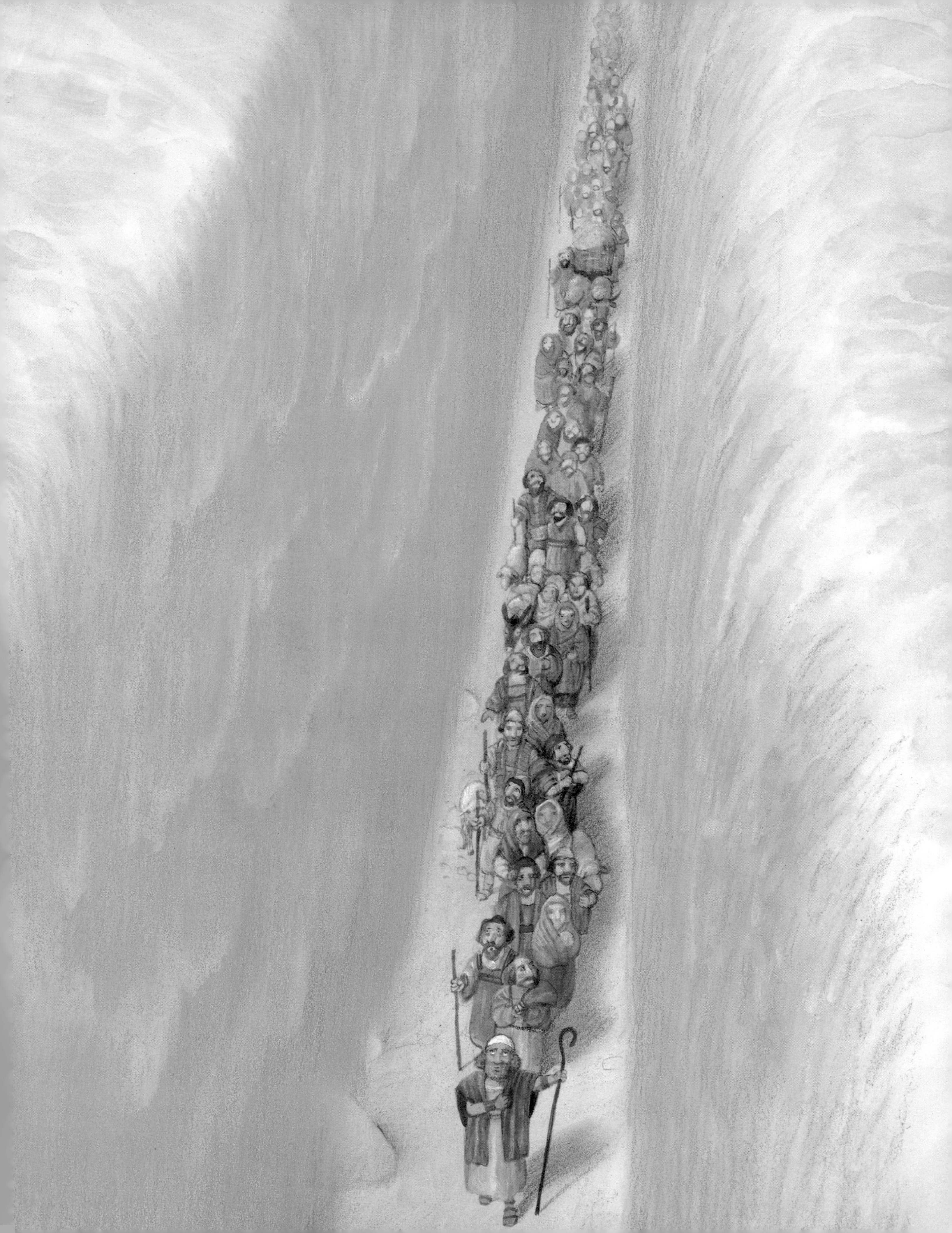

The Egyptians chased after them
with their horses, their chariots, and their riders.
But God told Moses to stretch out his hand once again,
and the sea closed up.
Of the pharaoh's army, nothing remained.

The children of Israel began to sing,
"Who is like you, O Lord, you who are holy?
You stretch out your hand, you make the wind blow,
you swallow horse and rider,
and you lead your people to the land
you have promised them."

The Hebrews traveled in the wilderness a long time,
and they came to the foot of Mount Sinai.
Sinai trembled and a cloud of smoke covered it,
for the Lord had descended upon the mountain.
From the cloud God called to Moses.

Moses climbed up, and God spoke to him, saying,
"I am the Lord your God
who brought you out of the land of Egypt,
and you shall have no other gods but me!
You shall not make statues for worship.
You shall not misuse the name of God.
You shall make the seventh day of the week
a holiday for rest and prayer.
You shall respect your father and mother.
You shall not kill.
You shall not take someone else's husband or wife.
You shall not steal.
You shall not unjustly accuse anyone.
You shall not covet what your neighbor has.
I give you these commandments
to bring to my people,
and I will be your God forever!"

Moses stayed on the mountain
forty days and forty nights.
And God gave him these commandments
written on tablets of stone.

At the foot of the mountain, the Hebrews were waiting.
Moses had been gone a long time.
They called Aaron, Moses' brother, and they said to him,
"Let us make a god we can see,
because Moses is not coming back
and we do not know what has happened to him."
They gathered all their jewelry and gave it to Aaron,
who melted the gold and cast from it a statue of a calf.
He built an altar in front of the statue,
and the people offered sacrifices.
They began to eat and drink, to dance and sing.

Just then, Moses came
down the mountain.
When he saw the golden calf,
he became very angry.
He threw down the stone tablets
on which God had written,
and they shattered on the ground.
The next day, Moses said,
"You have committed a great sin.
But now I will go back to the Lord
and ask him to forgive you."
The Lord said, "My angel will lead you
to the Promised Land.
But when the time comes for punishment,
I shall punish these people,
for they have sinned."

Moses went back up the mountain,
and God said to him, "Go, lead my people
to the land I have promised
to Abraham, Isaac, and Jacob,
to Sarah, Rebekah, and Rachel!"
God also said,
"Carve two new tablets of stone,
and on them I shall again write
my commandments.
I shall go among my people,
and for them I shall work miracles."

When Moses came down from the mountain
with the new tablets of stone,
his face was streaming with light
for he had spoken with God.

Young David and Goliath the Giant

In the time of King Saul,
the Philistines made war on the people of Israel.
And in the army of the Philistines was the giant Goliath.
His helmet was bronze, his breastplate was bronze,
and even the armor on his legs was bronze.

Goliath shouted to the soldiers of Israel,
"Let one man come to fight me.
If he wins, you will be our conquerors;
if he loses, you will be our slaves!"

Goliath shouted these words at the army of Israel
morning and evening for forty days.
Saul and his soldiers were terrified
at the sight of this huge man.

Now in that land, in Bethlehem,
there lived a man named Jesse who had eight sons.
The three oldest sons were soldiers
in the army of Israel.
The youngest, David, was a shepherd
who watched over his father's flock.

Jesse said to David,
"Go, bring your brothers this bread and cheese.
Then come back and tell me if they are well,
for they are in the valley with the army of Israel."

When David came to the valley,
he saw the two armies facing each other.
He saw Goliath come forward
and heard the words he was shouting.
The Israelites told David,
"The king will heap great riches
on the man who kills this giant!"

David went to find King Saul and told him,
"I will fight the giant Philistine
who believes he is mightier than our God!
I am only a young shepherd,
but when the lion and the bear
try to take a sheep from me,
I fight them,
and God protects me from their claws."
And Saul said, "Go, and may the Lord be with you!"

Saul gave David his helmet
and breastplate, but they were so heavy
he could not move.
He took them off and went down to the stream.
There he chose five smooth stones
and put them in his shepherd's pouch.
Then David walked toward the Philistine
with his sling in his hand.

The giant laughed when he saw him.
But David cried out,
"It is not by lance or sword
that our God gives victory!"

David took a single stone
and hurled it with his sling.
The stone struck Goliath on the forehead,
and he crumpled to the ground, dead.

The soldiers of Israel rushed forward
with a great war cry, and the army
of the Philistines fled before them.

The Great King Solomon

After the death of Saul,
David was anointed king of Israel.
And when David in turn died,
his son Solomon became king.

One night, God appeared to Solomon in a dream
and said to him, "Ask me what you will,
and I will give it to you."
Solomon answered, "O Lord,
you have made me king
in the place of my father, David.
I am ruler over many people,
so many they are uncountable!
I ask you for wisdom,
the wisdom to choose good
and reject evil.
Otherwise, how will I know how to govern
so great a people?"

Solomon's answer pleased God.
God said to him,
"Because you have not asked for riches,
or long life, or victory in war,
I give you wisdom such as no one has had before
and no one shall ever have again.
And you shall be a great king,
a king among kings!"

One day, two women came to Solomon
asking for justice.
One of them said to the king, "My lord,
this woman and I live in the same house.
And each of us has had a baby.
But her baby died last night,
and while I was sleeping
she took my son
and in his place left her dead son."
The other woman cried, "That's not true!
My son is alive, and hers is dead!"
And they shouted and argued before the king.

Solomon said, "Bring a sword
to cut the living child in two,
and give half to one woman
and half to the other!"
The first woman cried,
"Yes, let's divide him
so he won't be hers or mine!"

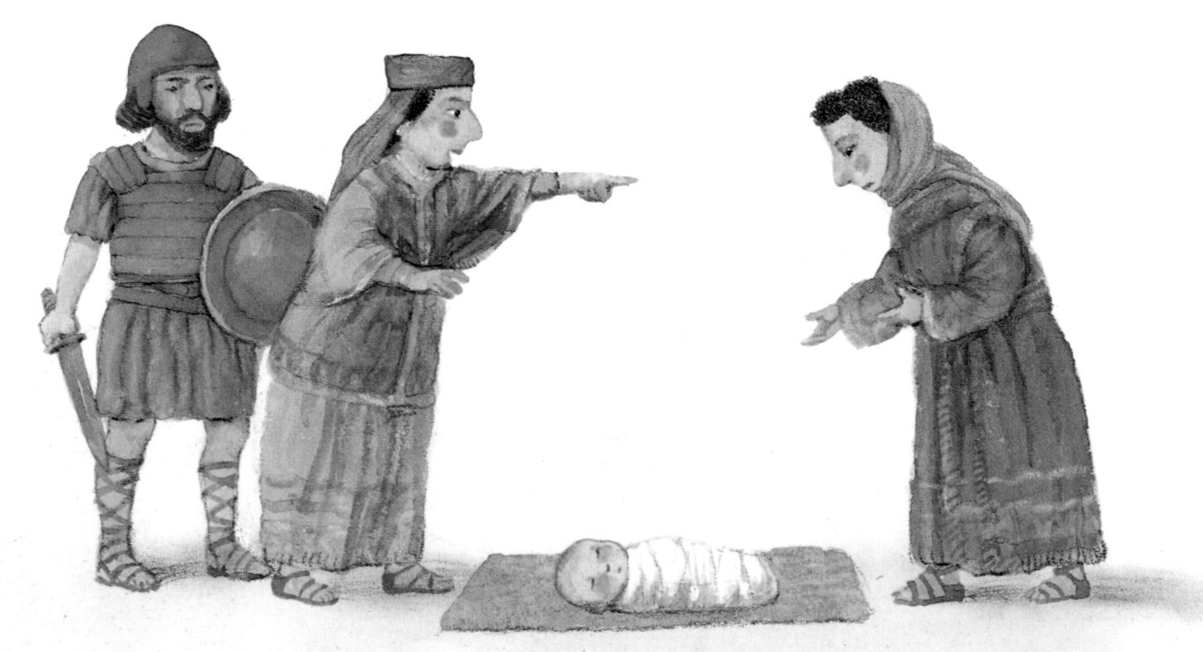

But the second woman begged,
"Please, my lord, don't kill the baby!
Let that woman have him!"
Then Solomon declared,
"This one is the mother.
Let the living child be given to her!"

Throughout Israel and all the surrounding lands,
people spoke of the wise judgment of the king.
And they held Solomon in high regard
because his wisdom came from God.

Solomon built for the Lord
a huge and magnificent temple
in the city of Jerusalem.
And God said to him, "As you are faithful to me,
so shall I be faithful to you.
I shall dwell among the children of Israel
and never abandon my people."

The Story of Jonah

There was in those days a city so big
it took three days to walk across it.
The city was called Nineveh,
and its people had become so wicked
that God decided to send them a warning.

God spoke to Jonah, saying,
"Go to Nineveh, that great city,
and tell all its people
that I have had enough of their evil ways!"
But Jonah did not want to do what
God had told him to do.
He boarded a ship
to flee from the Lord.

Then God whipped the sea with a wind
so wild that the ship threatened to sink.
Jonah said to the sailors,
"This storm arose because of me,
because I fled from my God.
Throw me into the sea
and the waves will cease their raging."
So the sailors threw Jonah into the sea,
and the storm stopped.
Then God sent a huge fish
to swallow Jonah.

Jonah stayed three days and three nights
in the belly of the fish,
and he prayed to the Lord, saying,
"You have cast me into the depths of the sea.
Waves pass over me and
weeds wrap round my head.
But my prayers rise up to you,
and from the land of death
you shall raise me, O Lord my God!"

God spoke to the fish,
and it spat Jonah out onto the shore.
Jonah rose to his feet
and went to Nineveh, the great city.
He walked the streets, shouting,
"In forty days, Nineveh shall be destroyed!"

The people of Nineveh believed the word of God.
The king himself rose from his throne.
They all covered themselves with ashes
to show they were sorry
and promised to do no more wrong.
Then God had mercy on the people of Nineveh,
and did not punish them
after all.

Daniel and the Lions

In those days, Darius, the king of Persia,
ruled Babylon and all the surrounding lands.
Darius favored Daniel, a young Israelite,
for Daniel was very wise
and knew how to explain dreams.
But the ministers at court were jealous of him
and tried to find a way to have him killed.
They convinced Darius to pass a law saying
that people must pray to the king only.
But Daniel continued to pray to God.
One day the ministers caught him
praying in his room.

At once they went to the king, saying,
"In our land, there is a law
forbidding anyone to pray to a god.
For are not you yourself our god, great king?"
Darius answered, "Truly, that is our law."
Then the ministers said to him,
"Well then, Daniel the Israelite disobeys you,
for he prays to his God in his room.
Therefore, according to our law,
he must be thrown into the lions' den!"

Darius was sad and angry, for he loved Daniel.
He looked for a way to save him
but found none.
Daniel was thrown into the lions' den.
Then Darius cried out,
"I cannot help you, Daniel,
but the God to whom you pray will protect you!"

The king returned to his palace,
but he could neither eat nor sleep.
At the first hint of dawn he rose and ran to the den.
"Daniel, Daniel," he called,
"Has your God saved you from the lions?"
And from deep in the den, Daniel answered,
"Great king, my God sent an angel
to seal the lions' jaws.
They have not hurt me,
just as I have hurt no one."

Overcome with joy, Darius pulled Daniel from the den.
Darius had the accusers thrown in instead,
and the lions devoured them.
Then the king ordered that throughout his realm
the God of Daniel be worshiped—
the living God who saves from harm
those who believe in him.

The Word of the Prophet Isaiah

The great prophet Isaiah said,
"Share your bread with the hungry;
bring poor people into your home.
Give clothing to the needy,
and do not ignore your own family.
Then God will rejoice with Jerusalem
and be happy with her people.
There will be no more weeping.
People will build houses and live in them.
People will plant gardens and enjoy their fruit."

He proclaimed,
"A descendant of David shall be born one day.
On him the spirit of the Lord shall rest.
And the wolf shall dwell with the lamb,
and the leopard shall lie down with the kid.
The child shall play with the snake,
and no one shall do evil.
For the love of God shall fill the earth
as water fills the sea."

Stories from
The New Testament

Mary of Nazareth

In the fullness of time, God sent the angel Gabriel
to Mary, a young woman
living in the town of Nazareth, in Galilee.
She was engaged to Joseph,
a descendant of King David.
Gabriel came to her and said,
"Greetings, Mary, full of grace,
for God is with you!"

Upon hearing these words, Mary was troubled.
But the angel said, "Do not fear!
You shall bear a son and you shall name him Jesus.
He shall be king
and he shall reign forever and ever!"

Mary replied,
"But how can this be, since I am not married?"
The angel said,
"The Holy Spirit shall come upon you
and the power of God shall cover you with its shadow.
And so your child shall be called
the Son of God!"
Mary then said,
"I shall trust in the Lord.
May it happen as you have said!"

A Cradle in a Manger

About that time, Augustus, the emperor of Rome,
commanded that a count be made
of all the people in his empire.
Each man was to go back to his hometown
to register his family.
So Joseph went to Bethlehem in Judea
with Mary, his wife, who was with child.
And there, in Bethlehem,
Mary gave birth to her baby.
She wrapped him in swaddling clothes
and laid him in the manger of a stable,
because the inn had no room for them.

Shepherds Keeping Watch

There were shepherds nearby
keeping watch over their flocks through the night.
The angel of the Lord appeared to them,
and the light of God shone around them.
The angel said to the shepherds,
"Do not be afraid!
I bring you news of great joy,
joy for all people.
For a savior is born to you this day
in Bethlehem, in the city of David.
He is Christ, the Messiah, the Lord.
This is how you will know him: he is a newborn baby
wrapped in swaddling clothes, lying in a manger."

All at once, angels' voices
filled the sky, saying,
"Glory to God in the highest,
and peace on earth through God's love!"

The shepherds said to each other,
"Let us go quickly to Bethlehem to see
all that has happened!"
And there they found Mary and Joseph,
and the baby lying in the manger.

Afterward they returned, praising God.
They told everyone what they had seen,
and all who heard them were filled with wonder.

A Star in the Sky

During those years, Herod was king of the Jews.
There came to Jerusalem wise men
from the East, known as Magi.

The Magi asked,
"Where is the king of the Jews,
the child who has just been born?
We have seen his star appear in the sky
and have come to bow down before him."

Herod was greatly disturbed.
He called together his chief priests and scholars
and asked if they knew
the birthplace of the Messiah.
They answered, "In Bethlehem, in Judea,
as the prophet has said."
Herod summoned the Magi in secret
and said to them,
"Go to Bethlehem and find the child.
When you have found him, bring me word,
so that I, too, may go honor him."

The Magi went on their way.
The star they had seen in the East
kept moving before them,
until it stopped over the place
where the infant was.

The Magi were filled with joy.
They entered and found
the child with his mother, Mary.
They bowed down before him,
and gave him gifts of gold,
frankincense, and myrrh.

The Flight into Egypt

That very night,
the angel of the Lord appeared to the Magi in a dream
and told them not to go back to Herod.
And so they returned to their country
by a different way.
The angel of the Lord also appeared to Joseph
and said, "Rise, take the child and his mother.
Go into Egypt and stay there
until the Lord tells you to return,
for Herod is going to search for the child,
in order to kill him."

The Slaughter of the Children

When Herod realized
that the Magi would not return,
he flew into a terrible rage.
He was afraid that the new king
would come to take his place,
and so he ordered that all baby
boys in Bethlehem be killed.
On that day, weeping and wailing
were heard throughout the land.

The Return to Nazareth

After the death of Herod,
the angel of the Lord appeared in a dream
to Joseph in Egypt. The angel said,
"Rise, take the child and his mother,
and return to the land of Israel,
for he who wished to harm the child is dead."
Joseph came back with Mary and Jesus,
and settled in the town of Nazareth,
in Galilee.

Jesus in the Temple

Each year,
Joseph and Mary traveled to Jerusalem
for the great Passover celebration.
When Jesus was twelve,
he went with them,
and after the holiday he stayed in Jerusalem,
though his parents did not know it.
Joseph and Mary traveled for a day,
thinking that Jesus was traveling with friends.
But when they discovered Jesus was not with them,
they went back to Jerusalem.

After three days of searching,
they found him in the temple.
Jesus was sitting among the teachers of religion.
He was listening to them and asking questions,
and all were amazed at his intelligence.

Mary and Joseph were astonished.
Mary said to Jesus,
"My child, why have you done this?
Your father and I were worried!"

Jesus answered, "Why did you search for me?
Didn't you know I would be in my Father's house?"
But Joseph and Mary did not understand
what he was saying.

Jesus went back to Nazareth with his parents.
He grew in strength and wisdom, and he pleased God.
And Mary kept all these things in her heart.

John the Baptist

Years passed, and a man came
to live in the wilderness,
a prophet called John the Baptist.
The people of Jerusalem and
of all Judea came to him to be baptized,
to be washed in the waters of the
river Jordan as they confessed their sins.

John told them, "Someone will come—
someone much greater than I.
I baptize you in water,
but he will baptize you in the Holy Spirit."

One day, Jesus himself came
to be baptized by John.
When Jesus left the water,
he saw heaven open
and the Spirit of God descend upon him
like a dove.
From heaven came a voice, saying,
"You are my son, whom I love.
With you I am well pleased."
And the Spirit of God led Jesus
into the wilderness.

Begone, Satan!

Jesus stayed in the wilderness
for forty days, and after forty days
he was hungry.
Satan came to him and said,
"If you are the Son of God,
turn these stones into bread!"

Jesus answered,
"Man does not live by bread alone,
but by the word of God."

Satan led Jesus up to the roof of the temple,
and he said, "If you are the Son of God,
throw yourself down, and the angels
will catch you in their hands!"

Jesus answered, "Do not test God!"

Satan then brought Jesus
to the top of a high mountain,
where he could see all
the kingdoms of the world.

And Satan said to him,
"I will give you all that you see,
if you will fall at my feet and worship me."

Jesus answered, "Begone, Satan!
Only God is to be worshiped!"
Then the devil left him,
and angels came to serve him.

The First Disciples

Jesus returned to Galilee.
As he walked along the seashore,
he saw two fishermen casting their nets.
They were Simon and his brother Andrew.
Jesus said to them, "Follow me,
and I will make you fishers of men and women."
Simon and Andrew dropped their nets
and followed him.

A little farther on,
Jesus saw James and his brother John.
He called to them,
and James and John also left their nets.
Simon, whom Jesus called Peter,
and Andrew, James, and John
were Jesus' first disciples.
They became his close companions.

Later, Jesus also chose
Thomas, Matthew, Philip,
Bartholomew, and Thaddeus,
then another James and another Simon,
and Judas, who would betray him.

The Best Wine

Jesus and his disciples were invited
to a wedding at Cana, in Galilee.
His mother, Mary, was also there.

By the middle of the meal,
all the wine had been drunk.
Mary said to Jesus,
"There is no more wine!"
Jesus replied,
"What do you want me to do, Mother?
My time has not yet come."
Then Mary told the servants,
"Do whatever he tells you!"

There were six large stone jars,
which held twenty-five gallons each.
Jesus said to the servants,
"Fill the jars with water."
The servants filled them to the top.
Jesus said, "Now, draw some out
and bring it to the master of the house."

The master of the house tasted
the water that had become wine
and said to the bridegroom,
"Usually the good wine is served first.
Then, after everyone has drunk freely,
the poorer wine is served.
But you have kept the best wine for last!"
This was the first of Jesus' signs,
and his disciples believed in him.

New Words

Jesus began to travel
across the land, telling everyone that
the kingdom of God was close at hand.
A large crowd followed him wherever he went.
Sick and frail people were brought to him,
and he cured them.

One day, he sat on a mountain,
and he spoke to the people who
had come to listen to him
in words that had never before been heard.

He said,
"Blessed are the poor in spirit,
for theirs is the kingdom of heaven.
Blessed are those who mourn,
for they shall be comforted.
Blessed are the meek,
for they shall inherit the earth.
Blessed are those who hunger
and thirst for justice,
for they shall be satisfied.
Blessed are the merciful,
for they shall receive mercy.
Blessed are the pure in heart,
for they shall see God.
Blessed are the peacemakers,
for they shall be called the children of God.
Blessed are those who are made to suffer
in the cause of justice,
for theirs is the kingdom of God."

Children of God

Jesus said to those who listened to him,
"You are the salt that seasons the earth.
You are the light that brightens the world.
Act with love even toward
those who wrong you,
and you will truly be the children
of God, who makes the sun rise
on both the wicked and the good,
and who lets the rain fall
on both the just and the unjust.
For if you love only those who love you,
what is unusual about that?
Anyone could do as much."

The House on the Rock

Jesus also said,
"Whoever listens to my words
and does what I say
is like the wise man
who built his house on a rock.
The rain fell, the winds blew,
and his house stood firm.
It was built on solid rock.

But whoever hears my words
and ignores them
is like the foolish man
who built his house on sand.
The rain fell, the winds blew,
and his house came tumbling down."

Jesus Calms the Storm

One day, as evening was falling,
Jesus got into a boat with his disciples
to cross a lake.
Without warning, a great gale sprang up.
The waves broke against the boat with such force
that it began to fill with water.

As for Jesus, he was lying down in the stern,
asleep, with his head on a cushion.
His disciples shook him, saying,
"Wake up! We're sinking!"

Jesus got up. He called to the wind
and the waves, "Be still!"
At once the wind dropped,
and a great calm followed.
Jesus said, "Why are you so frightened?
Have you no trust in me?"
Filled with awe, they
asked each other,
"Who can this Jesus be?
Even the wind and the sea obey him."

A Cripple Walks

One day, the people of Capernaum
learned that Jesus had come to their town,
and a crowd gathered in the house
where he was staying.
Some men came
carrying a crippled man on a stretcher,
but the crowd was so tightly packed
they could not get through.
So they clambered onto the roof
and made a hole.
Then they lowered the stretcher
down until it was in front of Jesus.

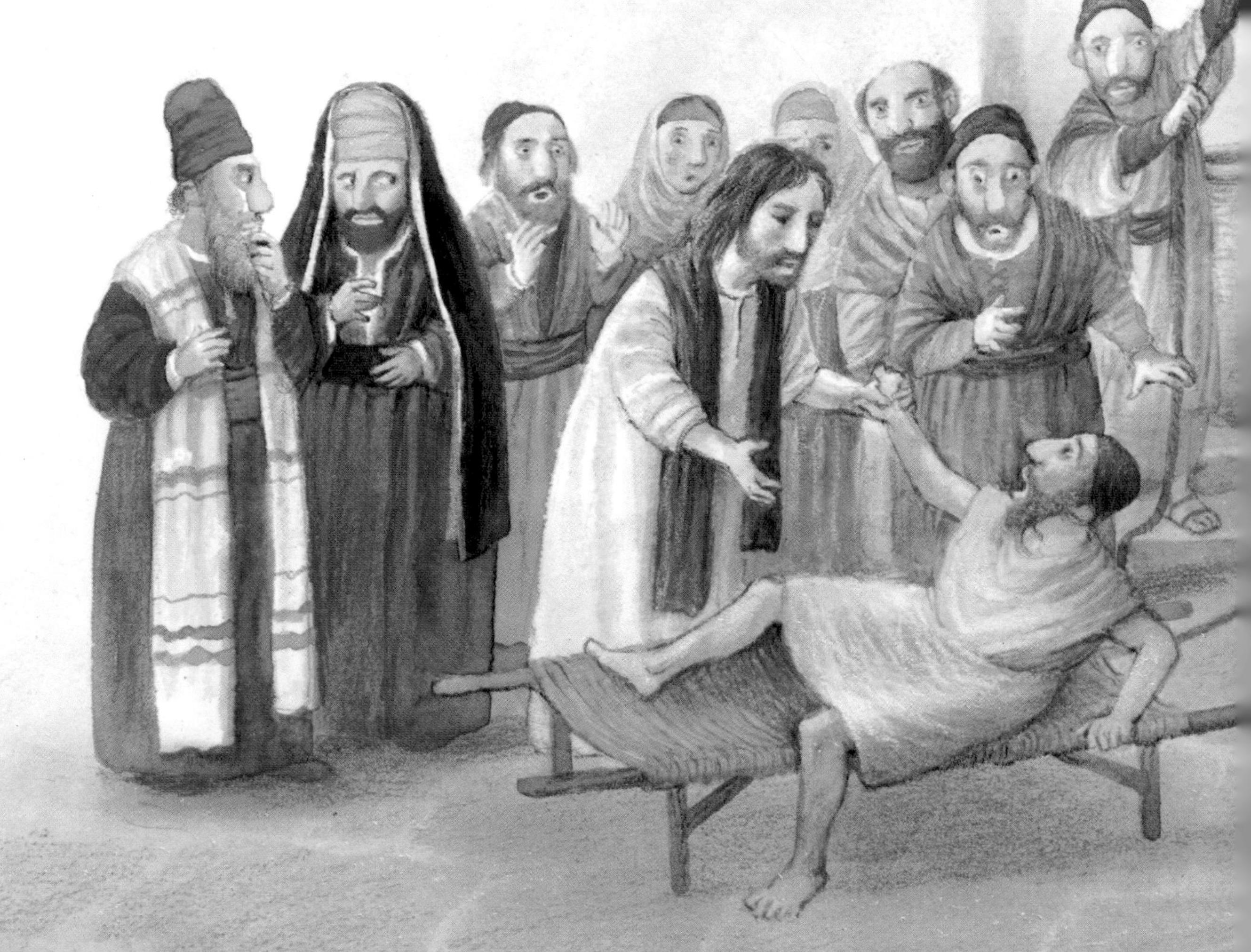

Jesus was touched by their faith.
He said to the crippled man,
"Your sins are forgiven."

Now there were in the crowd
some teachers of religion
who thought to themselves,
"What right has he to say this?
He is committing blasphemy.
Only God has the power to forgive sins!"

Jesus knew what they were thinking.
He said to them, "In your opinion,
is it easier to say to a crippled man,
'Your sins are forgiven,' or to say,
'Rise and walk'? I will prove to you
that I have the power to forgive sins."
And turning to the crippled man, he said,
"Rise, pick up your stretcher, and go home!"
Thereupon the man rose, picked up his stretcher,
and walked out before their eyes.

Like a Mustard Seed

Jesus said,
"The kingdom of God
is like a mustard seed,
the tiniest seed
that a man plants in his garden.
But when the seed grows,
it becomes the greatest of herbs,
and the birds come
to make their nests in its branches."

He also said,
"The kingdom of God is like yeast.
A woman making bread
takes but a tiny pinch
and mixes it
into a bowl of flour.
The dough then rises
into a fine loaf of bread."

Jesus and the Children

Many people brought
their children for Jesus to bless.
But his disciples were keeping them away.
When Jesus saw this, he was angry.

He told them,
"Let the children come to me,
for the kingdom of God belongs
to those who resemble them.
I tell you truly,
no one may enter the kingdom of God
who does not welcome it
with the heart of a child."

Jesus took the children into his arms
and he blessed them.

Five Loaves and Two Fishes

About that time, Herod Antipas,
the son of King Herod,
imprisoned John the Baptist
and then had him beheaded.
When Jesus learned of this,
he got into a boat
and went off by himself
towards the far side of a lake.

But a crowd of people from all over
went around the lake on foot.
When Jesus stepped ashore,
he found the people waiting for him.
He saw their suffering, and he cured their sickness.

When evening came, his disciples said to him,
"This place is a wilderness.
It is getting late,
and these people have nothing to eat."
Jesus answered,
"Then give them something to eat."
They said, "We have five loaves of bread
and two fishes, and there are more than
five thousand people here."
Jesus told the people to sit on the grass.
He took the bread and fishes,
blessed them, and broke them in pieces.
Then he told his disciples to share them out.
All present ate until they were full,
yet, at the end, twelve baskets still lay heaped
with the leftover pieces.

Like the Sun

Many priests and teachers of religion
were disturbed by Jesus,
because he spoke of God
as no one had before,
and people were flocking
to listen to him.

Jesus said to his disciples,
"Soon we shall go to Jerusalem.
There I must suffer and die,
and I shall rise on the third day."
But his disciples did not
understand what he meant.

Soon after, Jesus brought
Peter, James, and John
to the top of a high mountain.
There, his face shone like the sun,
and his clothes blazed with light.
Then two men appeared:
Moses and Elijah.

A voice spoke from heaven, saying,
"This is my Son, whom I love.
Listen to him!"
The disciples of Jesus fell
to the ground,
trembling with fear.
But Jesus came near them and said,
"Rise. Do not be afraid!"

While they were climbing
back down the mountain,
Jesus said to them,
"Do not tell anyone what you have seen
until the day I rise from the dead."

Zacchaeus Who Was Too Short

Jesus was passing through the city of Jericho.
People crowded around him,
bumping into each other.
Zacchaeus, a rich and dishonest tax collector,
wanted to see who Jesus was.
He was too short to see over the other people
and could not come closer because of the crowd,
so he ran ahead and climbed a tree.
Jesus lifted up his eyes and said,
"Climb down, Zacchaeus.
I would like to stay at your house today."

Zacchaeus climbed down from the tree.
Joyfully, he welcomed Jesus to his home.
And the people whispered to each other,
"Did you see that?
He has gone to stay with a dishonest man."
But Zacchaeus said to Jesus,
"Lord, I am going to give to the poor
half of all I own.
And those I have robbed,
I will repay four times over."
Then Jesus said, "Today
the grace of God has entered this house.
For I have come to save that which was lost."

On the Back of a Donkey

Jesus returned to Jerusalem.
When he reached the Mount of Olives,
he said to two of his disciples,
"Go to the entrance of the village,
where you will find a donkey's colt tied up.
Untie the colt and bring it to me."
The disciples brought the colt
and placed their cloaks on its back
for Jesus to sit on.
People threw branches
and spread their cloaks on the road.
They marched in procession, shouting,
"Hosanna, glory to God!
Blessed is he who comes in the name of the Lord!"

The Merchants in the Temple

Upon arriving in Jerusalem,
Jesus entered the temple.
In the courtyard were merchants
selling doves, rams, and bulls
for sacrifice.
There were also money changers.

Jesus made a whip out of rope
and chased the money changers, merchants,
and their animals from the temple.
He turned over the tables
and scattered the money, saying,
"My Father's house is a place of prayer,
but you have turned it into a den of thieves!"

Lazarus Who Was Dead

Jesus had a friend, Lazarus,
who was living in Bethany, in Judea,
with his sisters Martha and Mary.
Jesus loved all three very much.
One day, Jesus learned that Lazarus was sick,
and he decided to return to Judea.

But when he arrived in Bethany,
Lazarus had been dead for four days.
Martha ran to meet Jesus, and she said to him,
"If you had been here,
my brother would not be dead.
But I know that whatever you ask,
God will grant!"

Jesus answered, "I am the resurrection and the life.
Those who believe in me,
though they die, shall live!"

Mary in turn arrived and fell at Jesus' feet.
Then Jesus, too, was overcome by grief
and he wept.
He went to the cave that was used as a tomb
and had the stone that sealed the entrance removed.
Then he prayed, saying,
"Father, I know that you always hear me.
But I say it aloud
so that the people who follow me may believe
that it is indeed you who have sent me!"
Then Jesus cried in a strong voice,
"Lazarus, come out!"

And Lazarus, who had been dead,
walked living from the tomb.
Because of this, many people believed in Jesus,
and when the chief priests learned
what had happened, they were afraid.
That very day, they decided
to have Jesus killed.

For Thirty Pieces of Silver

Before the holiday of Passover,
the chief priests met.
They were looking for a way to arrest Jesus
and have him put to death.
Then Judas, one of the twelve disciples,
came to them, asking,
"How much will you pay me if I deliver him to you?"

They counted out thirty pieces of silver.
And from then on,
Judas looked for a chance
to deliver Jesus into their hands.

The Last Supper

On the first evening of Passover,
Jesus and his disciples were together
for the holiday meal.
While they were eating, Jesus said,
"One of you will betray me."
His disciples were full of sorrow,
and each asked in turn,
"Do you mean me, Lord?"
Finally, Judas asked,
"You don't mean me, do you?"
And Jesus answered, "Yes, you."

Then Jesus took bread and blessed it.
He broke it into pieces, saying,
"Take, eat, for this is my body."
Then he took the cup of wine and said,
"Drink, for this is my blood,
the blood I give so
that many may live."

In the Garden of Gethsemane

After the meal, they went to Gethsemane,
a garden on the Mount of Olives.
Jesus took Peter, James, and John aside.
A great anguish came over him,
and he went off by himself to pray.
Jesus fell to the ground, saying,
"Father, I am afraid.
But I trust in you.
Let all be done as you will."

Three times Jesus came back to his disciples,
and three times he found them asleep.
Finally, he said to them,
"Could you not stay awake for one hour with me?
Rise now, for those who plan to arrest me are near."

Just then, Judas arrived
with a large crowd
armed with swords and clubs.
Judas had told them,
"The one I kiss is the man.
Arrest him!"

Judas went to Jesus and kissed him.
Then the armed men seized Jesus.
And all the disciples fled.
They all abandoned him.

Jesus Is Condemned

Jesus was first brought before the high priest,
who asked him,
"Are you the Messiah, the Son of God?"
Jesus answered, "It is you who say so."
And all declared that this answer
was blasphemy and deserved death.

At dawn Jesus was led
to the palace of Pilate, the Roman governor,
who alone had the power
to condemn a prisoner to death.
Pilate questioned Jesus,
but Jesus made no answer.
Pilate was amazed.
He saw clearly that Jesus had done no wrong,
and he wished to free him.

But the crowd shouted, "Put him to death!
Put him to death!"
And Pilate was afraid.
He gave Jesus up to be nailed onto a cross,
for that was the way the Romans executed
criminals condemned to death.
Soldiers took Jesus out
and lashed him with a whip.
They spit in his face.
To make fun of him,
they dressed him as a king with a scarlet cape
and a crown of thorns.
Then they led him away to crucify him.

The Death of Jesus

The soldiers brought Jesus to Mount Golgotha,
and there they nailed him to a cross.
They also crucified two thieves,
one at his right, one at his left.
And the people passing by laughed at Jesus,
saying, "If you are the Son of God,
then climb down from the cross
and we will believe in you!"

Toward noon,
a great darkness fell over the earth.
At three o'clock Jesus cried out,
"Father, my spirit is in your hands!"
and he breathed his last.

That evening, two friends of Jesus
came to take his body down from the cross.
They wrapped it in a shroud
and placed it in a tomb cut into the rock.
They rolled a stone across the entrance.

INRI

The Empty Tomb

On the first day of the week,
at sunrise, three women headed for the tomb,
to embalm Jesus' body.
They said to themselves,
"Who will roll away the entry stone for us?"

But on arriving, they saw that
the stone had already been rolled away.
An angel in a dazzling robe was sitting in the tomb.
The angel said to them, "Why do you
look for the living among the dead?
Jesus who was crucified is no longer here.
He has risen. Go and tell his disciples!"

On the Road

That very evening,
two men were walking toward
the village of Emmaus,
discussing what had happened.
And Jesus was walking with them,
but they did not recognize him.
They told him what had happened
and how sad they were
because they had lost hope.
Jesus said to them,
"How slow your hearts are to believe!
Do you not understand
that the Messiah must pass through death
to give people life?"
And he began to explain to them
the words of the prophets.

When they drew near the village,
the two men said to Jesus,
"It is late. Night is falling. Stay with us."
And Jesus stayed with them for supper.
He sat down to eat; he took the bread;
he blessed it, broke it into pieces, and gave it to them.
Then their eyes were opened and they knew him.
But at that instant, Jesus disappeared.

The two said to each other,
"Didn't our hearts burn within us
at his words along the road?"
They set out at once for Jerusalem.
There they found the disciples of Jesus
who told each other,
"It is true. The Lord has risen!"

"I Am with You Forever"

More than once
Jesus appeared to his disciples.
He spoke to them.
He ate with them.
He told them,
"See, I am here with you
to the end of time."

One day when they were together,
Jesus said to them,
"Through me, the power of the Holy Spirit
will come upon you.
Then you will go and speak of me
in Jerusalem, in Judea, in Samaria,
and to the ends of the earth!"

At these words,
Jesus rose up before their eyes
and disappeared into a cloud.
Suddenly, two men in white
were there beside them.
They said, "Why do you stand here
staring at the sky?
Jesus shall return from heaven
the way you saw him leave!"

The Spirit of God

Fifty days after Passover,
the disciples of Jesus
met to celebrate the Pentecost.
Suddenly the house was filled
with the sound of a powerful wind,
and fiery flames sprang up
over each disciple's head.
Then they were filled with the Holy Spirit,
and they began to speak in foreign languages.

For the festival,
people had come to Jerusalem
from Mesopotamia and Pamphylia,
from Asia, Egypt, Rome, Libya,
and many other lands.
They were all amazed
to hear the people of Galilee
proclaim in their languages
the wonderful news:
Jesus who was crucified
has risen from the dead.
He is the Living God, the Lord.
He is with us forever and ever!

GLOSSARY

Aaron
Moses' brother. He sinned by making a golden calf for the Israelites to worship. 72

Abraham
Sarah's husband and the father of Isaac. God led Abraham and his family from Haran to Canaan. God appeared to Abraham in the form of three men at the entrance to his tomb. 42–48, 50, 53, 74

Adam
The first man. He was Eve's husband. Adam and Eve lived in the Garden of Eden until they ate the fruit of the tree of knowledge. 20–28

Andrew
One of Jesus' twelve disciples. He was Peter's brother. 114

angels
God's heavenly messengers. *Angel* comes from the Greek word *angelos*, meaning "messenger." 48, 53, 92, 96, 99, 104, 106, 112, 113, 153

anoint
To dedicate someone for service to God, usually by pouring a small amount of oil on the head. 80

Augustus
The emperor of Rome at the time of Jesus' birth. Augustus was also known by the name Octavian. 98

babble
To say things other people cannot understand. To talk nonsense. 40

Babel
The city where a tall tower was built to reach heaven. 38–40

Babylon
A city in ancient Persia. The ruins of Babylon are found in Iraq. King Darius was ruler over all of Persia during the time of the prophet Daniel. 90

Bartholomew
One of Jesus' twelve disciples. 114

Bethany
A town several miles outside of Jerusalem. Lazarus lived there with his sisters, Mary and Martha. 138

Bethlehem
A town near Jerusalem where Jesus was born. King David was also born in Bethlehem. 76, 98, 99, 100, 103, 105

blasphemy
Action or speech showing disrespect to God. 125, 147

breastplate
A piece of armor, usually metal, that protects a warrior's chest. 75, 78

Cana
The place in Galilee where Jesus performed his first miracle: turning water into wine at a wedding. 116

Canaan
The Promised Land to which God led Abraham. Canaan is located in modern-day Israel. 42

Capernaum
A region on the Sea of Galilee where Jesus performed many miracles. Capernaum is located in modern-day Israel. 124

cast
To heat metal until liquid and then pour into a mold to make an object of a certain shape. 72

chariot
A small, two-wheeled, horse-drawn vehicle used in ancient times. 66, 68

Christ
The title given to Jesus by God. It comes from *christos,* a Greek word meaning "the anointed one." 99

commandment
An order; a rule that must not be broken. The Ten Commandments are the rules given by God to Moses on Mount Sinai. 70, 74

covenant
An agreement. 36

covet
To long jealously for something belonging to another person. 70

crucify
To execute by nailing to a cross. 149, 150, 153, 159

Daniel
The prophet who was thrown into a den of lions and survived. He lived in Persia during the reign of King Darius, in the sixth century B.C. 90–92

Darius
The king of Persia during the time of the prophet Daniel. 90–92

David
The young Israelite who killed the Philistine giant Goliath and later became king over all Israel. David was the son of Jesse and the father of Solomon. 75–79, 80, 96, 99

devour
To eat up hungrily. 92

disciple
A person who followed Jesus to learn from him. 114, 116, 122, 127, 128, 130, 131, 134, 141, 142, 144, 146, 153, 155, 156, 158

embalm
To prevent decay of a body by treating it with preservatives. 152

Emmaus
A city west of Jerusalem. Jesus appeared to two of his disciples who were walking on the road to Emmaus. 154

Esau
The son of Isaac and Rebekah. Esau threatened to kill his twin brother, Jacob, so Jacob fled to a faraway country. 50

Eve
The first woman. Adam's wife. 20, 23–28

Gabriel
The angel who came to Mary and told her that she would bear a child named Jesus. 96

gale
A powerful storm. 122

Galilee
The northern region of ancient Palestine in what is today the state of Israel. Nazareth is in Galilee. 96, 106, 114, 116, 159

Gethsemane
A garden on the Mount of Olives where Jesus went to pray after the Last Supper. Judas betrayed him there. 144

God
The Being perfect in power, wisdom, and goodness whom people worship as the creator and ruler of the universe.

Golgotha
The name of the hill just outside Jerusalem where Jesus was crucified. It means "the place of the skull." 150

Goliath
The Philistine giant whom David killed. 75–79

Ham
One of Noah's three sons. 30

Haran
The place where Abraham and his family lived before they began their trip to the Promised Land. Haran is located in modern-day Iraq. 42

Hebrew
A member of the people of Israel. Also, the language the Israelites spoke. 54–66, 70, 72

helpmate
Companion and helper. 23

Herod
The king of Judea at the time of Jesus' birth. King Herod had all the male children in Bethlehem killed. 102–6, 128

Herod Antipas
The son of King Herod. Herod Antipas imprisoned John the Baptist and had him beheaded. 128

Holy Spirit
The Spirit of God. After Jesus ascended into heaven, he sent the Holy Spirit to fill the hearts of all who believed in him. 96, 110, 156, 158

Horeb, Mount
The mountain on the Sinai Peninsula where Moses saw the burning bush. Mount Horeb is often thought to be the same as Mount Sinai. 58

Hosanna
A Hebrew word that is an exclamation of praise to God. It means "Save us, we pray." 134

Isaac
Abraham's son and the father of Jacob and Esau. 45–48, 50, 53, 74

Isaiah
A great Hebrew prophet who lived around 700 B.C. His name means "The Lord saves." 94

Israel
The nation of people descended from Jacob. 53, 54, 58, 66, 69, 75, 76, 79, 80, 83, 84, 106

Israelite
A Hebrew person. A member of the nation of Israel. 90, 91

Jacob
Isaac's son, and Abraham's grandson. Jacob was Esau's twin brother. God changed Jacob's name to Israel, and he became the father of that nation. 50–53, 74

James
One of Jesus' twelve disciples. He was John's brother. 114, 131, 144

Japheth
One of Noah's three sons. 30

Jerusalem
The holy city of Israel. King David's palace was in Jerusalem. 102, 107, 110, 130, 134, 136, 155, 156, 159

Jesse
David's father. Jesse had eight sons and lived in Bethlehem. 76

Jesus
The Son of God. He is also called the Messiah, or Christ. 96–159

Jew
A Hebrew or Israelite. A believer in the religion of Abraham. 102, 103

John
One of Jesus' twelve disciples. He was James's brother. 114, 131, 144

John the Baptist
A prophet who proclaimed the coming of Jesus as the Messiah. John the Baptist was six months older than Jesus and was his cousin. 110, 128

Jonah
A prophet of God who was swallowed by a great fish. He traveled to the city of Nineveh to preach God's message. 86–89

Jordan River
The Jordan flows from the Sea of Galilee southward into the Dead Sea. Jesus was baptized in the Jordan. 110

Joseph
Jesus' earthly father. Mary's husband. 96, 98, 100, 104–8

Judas
The disciple who betrayed Jesus. 114, 141, 142, 146

Judea
The southern part of ancient Palestine. 98, 103, 110, 138, 156

kid
A young goat. 94

Lazarus
A friend of Jesus'. Jesus raised him from the dead. Lazarus lived in Bethany with his sisters, Mary and Martha. 138–40

Libya
In ancient times, a region on the northern coast of Africa. 159

livestock
Animals (cattle, sheep, horses, goats) kept or raised for use or pleasure. 61

locust
A type of grasshopper that often travels in vast swarms, eating all the vegetation in its path. 61

Lord
God.

Magi
The three wise men who came from the East to visit Jesus at his birth. 102–5

manger
A rough wooden trough that holds animal feed. 98, 99, 100

Mary
The mother of Jesus. Joseph's wife. 96, 98, 100, 103, 106–8, 116–17

Matthew
One of Jesus' twelve disciples. 114

meek
Patient, mild, humble. 118

memorial
An object or monument that serves to preserve the memory of a person or event. 53

Mesopotamia
The region in modern-day Iraq that is bounded by the Tigris and Euphrates Rivers. Mesopotamia is a Greek word meaning "between the rivers." 159

Messiah
Leader and savior. From the Hebrew word meaning "the anointed one." 99, 103, 147, 154

Midian
A desert region flanking the Gulf of 'Aqaba. Moses fled to Midian after he killed an Egyptian man. 58

money changers
Because the temple only accepted shekels, the local coin, worshipers had to go to money changers before they could pay their temple tax or buy sacrificial animals. Jesus threw the money changers out of the temple along with the animal sellers. 136

Moses
The prophet of God who led the people of Israel out of slavery in Egypt and into the Promised Land. As an infant, Moses was found floating in a basket in the Nile River; his name means "rescued from the waters." 54–74

Nazareth
The town in Galilee where Jesus grew up. 96, 106, 108

New Testament
The second half of the Bible written roughly between the years A.D. 50 and A.D. 95 (20 to 65 years after Jesus' life).

Nile
A great river that runs northward through Africa and Egypt. 54, 60

Nineveh
The ancient city to which Jonah traveled to preach God's message. Nineveh was located in what is now Iraq. 86, 89

Noah
He built a great ark. When the great flood came he lived inside the ark with his family and two of every kind of animal. 30–36

Old Testament
The first half of the Bible. It was written approximately between the years 1500 B.C. and 400 B.C.

Olives, Mount of
A hilly area just outside the city of Jerusalem. 134, 144

Palestine
The Middle Eastern region where Israel is located. In Jesus' day, Palestine was divided into Galilee, Samaria, and Judea.

Pamphylia
A region on the coast of modern-day Turkey. 159

Passover
A Jewish celebration to commemorate the night when God sent a plague on the firstborn of all people and animals in Egypt, but "passed over" the homes of the Israelites. Unleavened bread is eaten at Passover. 63, 107, 141, 142, 158

Pentecost
A Jewish feast known in Hebrew as Shavuot. During Pentecost the disciples of Jesus were filled with the Holy Spirit and spoke in foreign languages. Christians celebrate this event every year on the seventh Sunday after Easter. 158

perish
To die. 32

Persia
The ancient name for modern-day Iran. 90

Peter
One of Jesus' twelve disciples. He was originally called Simon. 114, 131, 144

pharaoh
The ruler of ancient Egypt. 54–68

Philip
One of Jesus' twelve disciples. 114

Philistines
A tribe that was often at war with Israel in biblical times. They lived on the western coast of ancient Palestine, in what is today Israel. 75, 78, 79

Pilate
The Roman governor at the time of Jesus' crucifixion. 148–49

proclaim
To announce; to declare in public. 94, 159

prophet
Someone to whom God speaks so that he or she might tell others. From a Greek word meaning "to speak forth." 94, 103, 110, 154

Rachel
The wife of Jacob. 74

Rebekah
Isaac's wife and the mother of Jacob and Esau. 74

rejoice
To feel joy or great delight. 45

resurrection
The act of rising from the dead to new life. 138

revere
To regard with great honor and respect. 48

Roman
Coming from or relating to Rome. The Roman Empire extended to Israel during the time of Christ. 148, 149

Rome
The city on the Italian peninsula that was the capital of the Roman Empire. Rome is the capital of modern-day Italy. 98, 159

sacrifice
To kill an animal as an offering to God (or a god). 46, 48, 72, 136

Samaria
The region in ancient Palestine that separated Judea and Galilee. 156

Sarah
Abraham's wife and the mother of Isaac. Sarah was a very old woman when she gave birth to Isaac. 42, 44–45

Satan
The devil. *Satan* comes from the Hebrew word for "adversary." 112–13

Saul
The first king of Israel, around 1000 B.C. Saul was king before David. 75, 78, 80

Shem
One of Noah's three sons. 30

shepherd's crook
A staff with a hooked end used by shepherds. 60, 66

shroud
A cloth used to cover the body of a dead person. 150

Simon
Another name for Peter, one of Jesus' disciples. Simon and his brother Andrew were both fishermen. 114

Sinai, Mount
A mountain in what is now Egypt, where Moses received the Ten Commandments from God. 70

Solomon
David's son. He was king of Israel after his father's death. Solomon was known for his great wisdom. 80–84

stable
A barn where livestock are kept. 98

stern
The rear part of a boat. 122

subside
To go down. 34